HOW TO
LISTEN

THICH NHAT HANH

**PARALLAX
PRESS**

BERKELEY, CALIFORNIA

Parallax Press
2236B Sixth Street
Berkeley, California 94710
parallax.org

Parallax Press is the publishing division of
Plum Village Community of Engaged Buddhism
© 2024 Plum Village Community of Engaged Buddhism
All rights reserved

Illustrations copyright © 2024 by Jason DeAntonis
Series design by Debbie Berne
Typesetting by Maureen Forys, Happenstance Type-O-Rama

Printed in Canada on FSC-certified paper

The material in this book comes from previously
published books and unpublished talks by
Thich Nhat Hanh

ISBN: 9780984627110
Ebook ISBN: 9780984627172

Library of Congress Cataloging-in-Publication Data is
available upon request

1 2 3 4 5 FRIESENS 29 28 26 25 24

CONTENTS

NOTES ON LISTENING

THE POWER OF LISTENING

Listening deeply to another is a form of meditation. We follow our breathing and practice concentration and we learn things about the other person that we never knew before. When we practice deep listening, we can help the person we're listening to remove the perceptions that are making them suffer. We can restore harmony in our partnerships, our friendships, our family, our community, our nation, and between nations. It is that powerful.

WE NEED TO TRAIN

We must listen to the other person so that they have a chance to express themselves. We try our best to listen, but after a few minutes we can no longer continue; their speech touches the pain, violence, and anger in us. At first, we vow that we will give the other person a chance, even if what they say is unjust or difficult to listen to. But because of the violence, fear, pain, and anger in ourselves, we cannot listen for more than five minutes; we want to react, shout back, or run away.

We have lost our capacity to listen with compassion, and we need to train so that we can listen again.

LISTENING TO OURSELVES

Before we can listen to another person well, we need to spend time listening to ourselves. Sometimes when we attempt to listen to someone else, we can't hear what they are saying at all because our own strong emotions and thoughts are too loud in us, crying out for our attention. We should be able to sit with ourselves, come home to ourselves, and listen to what emotions are rising up, without judging or interrupting them. We can listen to whatever thoughts come up as well, and then let them pass without holding on to them. When we've spent some time listening to ourselves, we can listen to those around us.

UNDERSTANDING OUR SUFFERING

When we listen deeply to ourselves, we can understand ourselves, accept ourselves, love ourselves, and start to touch peace. Perhaps we have not yet accepted ourselves because we don't understand who we are; we don't know how to listen to our own suffering. So, we must first of all practice listening to our own suffering. We must be with it, feel it, and embrace it in order to understand it and allow it to gradually transform. Perhaps our own suffering carries within it the suffering of our father, our mother, the whole line of our ancestors, or a whole country. Listening to ourselves, we can understand our suffering—the suffering of our ancestors, our father, and our mother—and we feel a sense of release.

COMING HOME WITH MINDFULNESS

When we stop the busyness of the mind and come back to ourselves, our suffering can seem very intense. This is because we are so used to ignoring it and distracting ourselves from the pain. With distractions, we may succeed in numbing ourselves for a little while, but the suffering inside wants our attention and it will fester and churn away until it gets it.

That's why the first practice is to stop running, come home to our bodies, and recognize our feelings of suffering—our anger, our anxiety, our fear. Suffering is one energy. Mindfulness is another energy that we can call on to embrace the suffering. The function of mindfulness is first to recognize the suffering and then to embrace it.

The practice is not to fight or suppress the feeling, but rather to cradle it with tenderness. When a mother embraces her child—even if she doesn't understand at first why the child is suffering—that energy of tenderness can already bring relief. If we can recognize and cradle the suffering while we breathe mindfully, there is relief already.

Your suffering is trying to get your attention, to tell you something, and now you can take the opportunity to listen.

A FAITHFUL FRIEND

In our daily life, we breathe, but we forget that we're breathing. Although our body is in one place, our mind is often in another. Paying attention to our in-breath and out-breath brings our mind back to our body. And suddenly we are there, fully present in the here and the now. This is called mindfulness of breathing, or conscious breathing. It's very simple, but the effect can be very great.

We don't need to control our breath. We feel the breath as it actually is. It may be long or short, deep or shallow. Regardless of our internal weather—our thoughts, emotions, and perceptions—our breathing is always with us, like a faithful friend.

NO LONGER A VICTIM

As we listen to our own suffering, we must let go of the idea that we are a victim of others. Our lack of self-esteem and our anger have been with us for a long time. These are big obstacles on our path of practice. We must recognize them. We must see that our suffering is our inheritance. This understanding alone will already help liberate us. We can say to our suffering, "I am here for you. I will take care of you and transform you." In this way, our tendency to blame others for our suffering, believing it's the other's fault, will fade naturally.

LIGHTEN YOUR SUFFERING

If we have insight and love, we will not suffer.
And if we have insight and love, it's because
we've listened to ourselves deeply. Perhaps
our suffering, our difficulties, have accumulated
over the years. We can now take advantage of
this opportunity to lighten our suffering—for
ourselves and for the generations who will
continue after us. That's why we must have the
time to sit peacefully and listen deeply.

SITTING PEACEFULLY, LISTENING DEEPLY

Sitting meditation is a way for us to return home and give full attention and care to ourselves. Every time we sit down, whether it is in our living room, at the foot of a tree, or on a cushion, we can radiate tranquility like the Buddha sitting on an altar. We bring our full attention to what is within and around us. We let our mind become spacious and our heart soft and kind. With just a few minutes of sitting in this way, we can restore ourselves fully. When we sit down peacefully, breathing and smiling with awareness, we have sovereignty over ourselves.

Sitting meditation is very healing. We can just be with whatever is within us, whether it is pain, anger, irritation, joy, love, or peace.

We are with whatever is there without being carried away by it. We let it come, let it stay, then let it go. We have no need to push, to oppress, or to pretend our thoughts are not there. Instead, we can observe the thoughts and images in our mind with an accepting and loving eye. Despite the storms that arise in us, we're still and calm.

Sitting and breathing, we produce our true presence in the here and the now and offer it to our community and to the world. This is the purpose of sitting: being here, fully alive and fully present.

ENJOYING OUR STEPS

Walking meditation is walking just to enjoy walking—it is not a means to an end. We do not put anything ahead of ourselves and run after it. We enjoy our steps with no particular aim or destination. We have already arrived.

Our mind tends to dart from one thing to another, like a monkey swinging from branch to branch without stopping to rest. Thoughts have millions of pathways, and they forever pull us along into the world of forgetfulness. If we can transform our walking path into a field for meditation, our feet will take every step in full awareness. Our breathing will be in harmony with our steps, and our mind will naturally be at ease.

STOPPING AND LISTENING TO THE BELL

A bell of mindfulness is a tool for helping us to arrive. It doesn't have to look like a typical bell. Any sound that reminds you to pay attention to your breathing can be a bell of mindfulness: the sound of the wind, the sound of a bird, even the sounds of cars or a baby crying. They are all a call from the Buddha to return to ourselves. Practicing with an actual bell from time to time is helpful, and once you can practice with a bell, you can practice with other sounds. We learn that it isn't a Buddha outside us who calls us back to ourselves, but our own Buddha within us.

When we listen to a bell, we stop every-thing. We stop walking, we stop moving, we stop talking; we not only quiet our mouths, but we also quiet our minds, and simply come back to our breathing and our body. We take that moment to really rest, check in with how our body is doing, and let go of any tension.

WHY AM I HERE?

When you sit in meditation, you may ask your-self, "Why am I here?" If you listen to yourself deeply enough, and if you listen to the bell of mindfulness deeply enough, the answer will reveal itself to you.

APPROPRIATE ATTENTION

When we hear the sound of a bell, we can place all our attention on that sound. We are practicing appropriate attention.

Buddhist teachings distinguish two kinds of attention: appropriate attention and inappropriate attention. When our mind is directed toward something beautiful, wholesome, or spiritual, it benefits our whole being, our whole consciousness. This is appropriate attention. If your attention is drawn to something violent or unwholesome, your mind may become filled with sorrow, anger, and prejudice. This is inappropriate attention. With mindfulness, we can practice appropriate attention, focusing on what is good and wholesome, and water the seeds of peace, joy, and liberation in us.

When we focus our mind on a wholesome object, we water the beautiful and wholesome seeds in us. We establish ourselves in the here and the now, we touch the depth of our being, and we receive healing and peace—that is what we call appropriate attention.

LISTENING WITH MINDFULNESS GIVES RISE TO CONCENTRATION AND INSIGHT

If we practice long enough, we are able to stop talking and thinking whenever we hear the bell. We come back to our breathing and we generate the energy of mindfulness, concentration, and insight.

The energy of mindfulness is the full awareness of the present moment. This energy carries within itself the energy of concentration. When you are mindful of something, whether that something is a flower, a friend, or a cup of tea, you become concentrated on the object of your mindfulness. The more you are mindful, the more concentrated you become—concentration is born from mindfulness. And if you are concentrated enough, the energy of concentration contains the energy of insight, wisdom. Mindfulness, concentration, and insight are the energies that make up the Buddha. These three kinds of energy can transform our habit energies and lead to healing and nourishment.

SILENCE COMES FROM YOUR HEART

Silence is something that comes from your heart, and not from the outside. If you are truly silent on the inside, then no matter where you find yourself, you can enjoy the silence. Silence does not mean that we don't talk or do things. Silence means there is an inner silence, our mind is not disturbed—there is no talking, no ruminating inside.

TRANSFORMING HABIT ENERGIES

"I am here" means I exist. I'm truly here because I'm not lost in the past, in the future, in my thinking, in the noise inside, or the noise outside. Thanks to the practice of mindful breathing, we can free ourselves from the noise in our heads and from our unhelpful or unbeneficial habit energies.

There is a strong energy in every one of us called "habit energy." We all have habit energies that make us say and do things we don't want. Intellectually, we may know that doing or saying a certain thing will cause a lot of suffering, but we do it anyway, and later we regret it. Once we say or do something, the damage is done; we cannot take it back.

You may vow not to repeat your mistake in the future, but the next time the situation presents itself, you end up doing the very same thing again. This is the power of the habit energies that your parents and ancestors may have transmitted to you.

Mindful breathing can help you recognize habit energy when it emerges. You don't have to fight that energy; you only have to recognize it as yours and smile to it. That is enough. You recognize it and smile to it, and then you are free. This is a wonderful way of protecting yourself and of protecting others.

OUR THOUGHTS PREVENT US FROM HEARING

Most of us have a radio constantly playing in our head tuned to the station Radio NST— Radio Nonstop Thinking. Most of this thinking is unproductive thinking. The more we think, the less available we are to what is around us. Therefore, we have to learn to turn off the radio and stop our thinking in order to fully enjoy the present moment.

THUNDERING SILENCE

In order to truly be, we must be free. Free from what? Free from thinking, free from anxiety, fear, and longing. When the noise within us disappears, there is the emptiness of sound. This kind of silence is extremely eloquent, extremely powerful; we call it "thundering silence." Against the background of this kind of silence, you hear very clearly.

Your heart is calling you; it is trying to tell you something, but you may not be able to hear it because your mind is so full of noise, of thoughts. But when you are able to quiet all the noise inside of you and establish silence— thundering silence— you begin to hear the deepest kind of calling from within.

NOURISHING OURSELVES

In the Buddha's teachings, sensory impressions are considered a kind of food. We "eat" with our six sense organs: our eyes, ears, nose, tongue, body, and mind. A television program is food; a conversation is food; music is food; art is food; billboards are food. When you drive through the city, you consume these things without your knowledge or consent. What you see, what you touch, what you hear is food.

These items of consumption can nourish understanding and compassion in us or they can be highly toxic. Many of them water seeds of craving, despair, and violence. If we don't know how to consume mindfully, the toxins of violence, despair, and craving penetrate right into the core of our being. It's not a problem of consuming less or more, but of mindful consumption.

When you hear the voice of someone who is full of compassion, full of understanding, patience, and love, you are consuming wholesome food. Once you learn how to nourish yourself with understanding and compassion, you too will be capable of producing wholesome and nourishing thoughts.

WHAT HAVE WE BEEN CONSUMING?

If we experience depression, the Buddha advises us to look deeply into our depression to find the source of nutriment we are feeding it with—nothing can survive without food. What have we been consuming? How and where have we been living? We may have consumed ideas, beliefs, thoughts, conversations, news, sounds, and images that have contributed to our depression. The Buddha said, "When you are able to see the source of nutriment that has brought something to be, you are already on the path of emancipation." It is important to cut off the source of nutriment so our depression can heal. We should not feed it anymore. Mindful consumption is crucial for self-protection, for our well-being, and for the well-being of our community.

INSIGHT IS BORN
FROM LISTENING

In the sutras, some people attained enlightenment after hearing a single Dharma talk given by the Buddha. They did not compare what they already knew with what the Buddha was saying. Instead, they simply opened their heart, allowing the rain of the Dharma to penetrate the soil of the mind. In that way, the seeds of awakening could sprout, which led to immediate insight.

Becoming enlightened is not a matter of theory, of ideas, or of thinking; it's a matter of insight. And insight is born thanks to deep looking and deep listening.

LETTING GO

When we listen to someone, we already have ideas about what is being said. We tend to bring up and compare what we already know with what we are hearing. If the two things are the same, we say, "Oh, that's right." We accept it. When we compare and we see that what's being said isn't the same as what we've already learned, we say, "Oh, that's wrong; I can't accept that." And in both cases, we learn nothing.

SEEDS OF UNDERSTANDING

What we are listening to can be the opposite of what we "know." And if we resist what we are hearing, it will not go into our heart; it will not serve any purpose.

When reading something or listening to something new, don't work too hard. Be like the earth. When the rain comes, the earth only has to open herself to receive the rain. Allow the rain of the Dharma to fall and penetrate the seeds that are buried deep in your consciousness. A teacher cannot give you the truth. The truth is already in you. You only need to open yourself up—body, heart, and mind—so that the teachings can penetrate the soil of your mind and water your own seeds of understanding and enlightenment. You only need to let the words enter you; the soil and the seeds themselves will do the rest of the work.

CREATING SPACE

When another person speaks—our father, our partner, our child, our teacher, a sibling—we should know how to listen to them. Knowing how to listen means that we give the person a chance; we allow what we hear to sink in. For that to be possible, we must create space in our heart and mind. If our teacup is already full, how can we pour in more? The teacup must have space, and we must have space, too.

Every one of us has lots of opinions, lots of views, and those opinions and views may be what we call wrong views—full of bias, prejudice, stereotypes, or wrong perception. But when we let go of our opinions and views— when we create space—then what others say can truly penetrate. So please empty yourself when you listen—that's the art of deep listening.

We fight each other, we kill each other, and we wage war, all because we don't know how to make space within ourselves or how to listen deeply. If we know how to do this, we stand a good chance of building peace and helping humanity.

A HEART LIKE A RIVER

According to the teaching of the Buddha, everyone has the seed of equanimity within themselves—the capacity to accept or embrace what is. Somebody says something that we do not like, and we suffer. But whether we suffer a lot or a little, or whether we suffer at all, depends on our heart's capacity to accept and embrace. If we practice, if we train, our heart's capacity will grow.

The Buddha once said, "Imagine someone stirred a handful of salt into a small bowl of water. Monks, do you think that the water would be drinkable?" And the monks said, "The water would be far too salty to drink." Then the Buddha said, "But if you were to throw the same handful of salt into the river, would the river water be drinkable?" And the monks said,

"Yes—the river is vast. The handful of salt could not possibly make the river water taste salty."

It is the same for us. If our heart is small, then unjust words will make us angry. If our heart is great, like the river, then those words will not have any effect on us. We can continue to smile, we can continue to be as free, peaceful, and joyful as we were before. Therefore, the practice of equanimity helps us to look deeply, to see the truth clearly, and to allow the heart of understanding and love in us to grow. Then our heart becomes like a river; people may throw twenty or thirty kilos of salt into it, but we will not suffer.

A HEART THAT EMBRACES ALL

When our heart is large, we embrace "friends" and "enemies" alike; we love them equally, and they are equally the object of our compassion. We can practice so that our heart grows larger all the time.

COMPASSION HEALS US

Compassion is the intention and capacity to relieve and transform suffering—in ourselves, in the other person, and in the world. To develop compassion, we need to practice mindful breathing, deep listening, and deep looking. In the same way that we recognize the suffering in ourselves, we can recognize and embrace the suffering in the people around us. Listening to the suffering, holding it, we aim to understand it. When we get in touch with our own suffering and start to understand it, the energy of compassion begins to arise. When the energy of compassion is born, it begins to heal us, heal the other person, and heal the world.

When I was a novice, I could not understand why, if the world was filled with suffering, the Buddha still had such a beautiful and peaceful smile. Why wasn't he disturbed by all the suffering? Later I discovered that it's because the Buddha had enough understanding, calm, and inner strength; that is why he wasn't overwhelmed by all the suffering around him or within him. He could smile to his suffering because he knew how to take care of it and transform it. We should be aware of suffering, but we should also retain our clarity, calm, and strength so that we can help transform the situation. The ocean of tears cannot drown us if compassion is there.

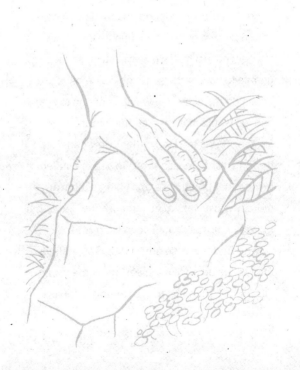

LISTENING TO A SUFFERING PERSON WITHOUT TAKING ON THEIR PAIN

If the other person does not know how to handle their own suffering, they will become the first victim of their suffering—we are only the second victim. If we were in their situation, unable to handle the suffering inside of us, we would do the same: we would continue to suffer, and we would make the people around us suffer, too. This is the kind of right view generated through mindfulness: when we see the suffering in the other person, we don't blame them anymore; we just want to help them suffer less. That means compassion has been born in us.

The Buddha once advised his son, Rahula, to practice being like the earth. People throw all kinds of things on the earth—from flowers to garbage—and the earth receives all of it with equanimity, without judgment. The earth has the power to transform all of these things. We can learn to practice with equanimity like Mother Earth. We can receive whatever someone says to us, without taking on their suffering.

THE CAPACITY TO OFFER WELL-BEING

There are people who are very pleasant to be with—just sitting near them, we feel their wonderful energy of love and well-being. A person who cultivates loving kindness is like that: their presence alone is refreshing and healing.

Loving kindness is the capacity to offer well-being and happiness. You cannot offer something that you do not have. With the practice of calming, looking deeply, and understanding, you allow the energy of loving kindness to grow within yourself; you are the first to profit from that energy. You experience bliss, solidity, freedom, and well-being, and your presence will naturally offer the person you are with that same kind of energy. Before you do or say anything, your presence can already make them happy, because in you there is the energy of loving kindness.

When we look deeply and understand, we can offer joy and happiness to the other person; we can give them what they really need.

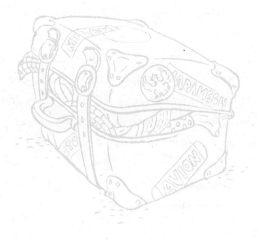

LISTENING WITH COMPASSION TO RELIEVE SUFFERING

Sometimes it only takes half an hour of listening to someone deeply for them to feel relief from their suffering. But you must be truly present, in the here and the now, with compassion in your heart. Whatever the other person says, even if it's untrue or comes from a wrong perception, even if it is full of bitterness, blame, and false accusations, as long as you can remain calm and open, it won't touch off anger and irritation in you. You will be protected by your own compassion and calm. You know you are listening with only one purpose in mind: to help the other person relieve their suffering.

If you interrupt and correct them, you'll turn the session into a debate and you will have missed the opportunity to help them. Later on, you may be able to help correct their wrong perceptions, but for now, you just listen with compassion and an open heart and mind.

BODHISATTVA ENERGIES

In Buddhism, the Bodhisattva Avalokiteshvara, or Kwan Yin, is skilled in the art of deep listening, and the Bodhisattva Manjushri has the capacity to look deeply. These bodhisattvas of deep listening and deep looking are inside us. When we practice looking deeply to understand someone's suffering, the Bodhisattva Manjushri is alive within us, and when we listen with compassion to understand the suffering and pain of the other person, the Bodhisattva Avalokiteshvara is also alive within us. It is not a question of believing in the existence of a god or of Bodhisattvas. The question is whether we have the capacity to touch the energy of compassion within us and express it in our manner of looking and listening deeply. We cultivate this capacity through continued practice.

KNOWING OUR LIMITS

To be heard by someone who can listen deeply is a most precious opportunity; it can bring great relief. But there are times when listening will not bring any relief, for example, when someone repeats things that water the negative seeds in both both of us. In this case, it isn't intelligent to continue listening.

If you don't feel that you can continue to listen with compassion, let the other person know. Ask your friend, "Dear one, can we continue in a few days? I need to renew myself. I need to practice so that I can listen to you in the best way I can." If you are not in good shape, you are not going to listen in the best way you can. Practice walking meditation, mindful breathing, and sitting meditation in order to restore your capacity for compassionate listening.

WATERING SEEDS

We can practice mindfulness in such a way that we can water the positive seeds within us and let the negative seeds rest. In Buddhist psychology, we use a circle divided in half to represent our consciousness. The upper half represents the mind and the lower level represents *store consciousness*, which contains the totality of all possible seeds—seeds of well-being as well as seeds of ill-being. Mind consciousness is like the living room, and store consciousness is like the basement.

When we water a seed with our awareness, it becomes energized and rises from store to the upper level, mind consciousness. Once in mind consciousness, it's no longer called a seed, but a mental formation.

In the depths of our consciousness there are beneficial seeds of love, compassion, joy, forgiveness, and so on. But there are also other seeds in store consciousness—anger, fear, despair, and trauma are all there.

CHANGING THE PEG

We should practice not to allow the unbeneficial seeds to manifest. We allow them to sleep quietly and peacefully down in store consciousness. If by chance the seed of anger, despair, jealousy, suffering, or trauma has already manifested as a mental formation, we do something to help it go back down to sleep as a seed in store consciousness. When a seed manifests in mind consciousness and stays there for a long time, the seed grows stronger at the base. So, if an unbeneficial mental formation manifests, don't allow it to stay too long.

One way to help it go back down is to invite a beneficial seed to come up and replace it. The Buddha uses the image of a carpenter's peg. To join two pieces of wood, the carpenter makes a hole in each one, aligns the holes, and drives in a peg. But if a peg becomes rotten or is no longer good, he changes the peg by using a new peg to drive out and replace the old one. Likewise, when an unbeneficial mental formation manifests, we should know how to replace it with a good one.

MAKE HAPPINESS A
REGULAR THING

Joy and happiness are always possible. We can create a feeling of joy, happiness, serenity, peace, self-fulfillment, or forgiveness by giving the beneficial things a chance to manifest. When something beneficial arises, we should try to keep it with us as long as possible, like a friend in our living room. The longer a beneficial seed stays in our mind consciousness, the stronger it will become. If the seeds of happiness and love have become strong, they will manifest by themselves; happiness becomes a regular, normal thing.

UNDERSTANDING IS THE FOUNDATION OF LOVE

When you love someone, you want them to be happy. But you make mistakes; your beloved suffers and so do you. If you don't look deeply and understand the person you love well enough—if you don't understand their difficulties, their pain, their deepest aspirations—it will be impossible for you to love them and make them happy.

Understanding is the foundation of love. That is why it is useful to ask your beloved, "Darling, do you think that I understand you well enough? I know that if I misunderstand you, I will make mistakes and make you suffer. Please tell me what is in your heart—tell me about your pain, your fear. I will try to listen."

HELPING OTHERS TO LISTEN WITH LOVING SPEECH

It is not so easy for people to express what is in their hearts. To help them feel at ease, you have to practice loving speech—speech that inspires joy and confidence—and encourage them with all your care and skillfulness. You do your best to create a safe environment where they can be assured that they will not be reprimanded, punished, or harassed when they speak their truth.

You should also be able to share your own suffering with others. You can help them to listen to you by using loving speech free of blame or bitterness. If you blame, accuse, or criticize them, they will have difficulty listening to you. If you tell them about your suffering from a place of compassion and understanding, it will help them to understand you.

LISTENING TO UNDERSTAND, UNDERSTANDING TO RECONCILE

If you listen with mindfulness to someone with whom you have a deep conflict, you'll recognize that they have suffered in almost the same way as you. As you listen, you see that they have the same fear, anger, and suspicion, and you begin to see them as a human being. And when you see them as a human being who is suffering, the desire to punish them dissolves; you begin to look at them with the eyes of compassion.

That is how you can transform yourself through the practice of compassionate listening. Now, looking at the other party, you suffer much less because you can see that they suffer, too. When you look at them with this awareness, they see the understanding in your eyes;

they feel you looking at them with love and not with suspicion, fear, or anger. Transformation takes place on both sides.

THE MIND OF LOVE

In Buddhism, we say that the deepest aspiration is bodhicitta, the mind of love. Giving rise to the mind of love, you give rise to a strong aspiration for peace, compassion, and understanding. "I vow to develop understanding and compassion so that I can become an instrument of peace and love, helping society and the world." With this kind of powerful volition, we can understand others in a way that they haven't yet understood themselves. This deep aspiration is connected to the realization that we are all interconnected; we inter-are— we are not separate selves. My happiness is your happiness, just as your suffering is also my suffering. Happiness and suffering are not an individual matter. It's through this insight of interbeing that we can really understand, we can really love.

INTERBEING

"Interbeing" means that nothing can be by itself alone, but can only inter-be with everything else. Suppose we look at a rose deeply, with mindfulness and concentration. Before long, we will discover that the rose is made of only non-rose elements. What do we see in the rose? We see the cloud, the rain, the sunshine, the soil, the minerals, the gardener. If we were to remove the non-rose elements, there would be no rose left. A rose cannot be by herself alone. A rose has to inter-be with the whole cosmos.

We can live our daily life seeing everything in the light of interbeing. Then we will not be caught in our small self or in the idea of a separate self. We will see our connection, our joy, and our suffering everywhere.

FREEING OURSELVES FROM COMPLEXES

We know that a superiority complex causes suffering both in ourselves and in others. An inferiority complex, or low self-esteem, is the root of many problems and mental illnesses. So, we may believe that equality is the best solution, yet the notion of equality is also the cause of a lot of suffering.

In political terms, we say that we have "the right to be equal" but looking deeply, we see that comparing ourselves with others—the comparison itself—is the root of our suffering. Believing "I am better than they are" is an expression of a superiority complex. "I am worse than they are, I cannot catch up with them" is an expression of an inferiority complex. However, believing "I am their equal; I am as good as they are" is also a complex—the equality complex. We should practice to recognize and free ourselves from all three complexes. All three bring us suffering.

NO COMPARISON

The Buddha teaches that there is no self; therefore, there is no comparison. When we don't compare anymore, happiness is there. We can say, "Darling, you are me and I am you. Your suffering is my suffering. Your happiness is my happiness." This deep insight—the insight of interbeing—is very important.

Looking deeply, you see that you only inter-are; you cannot *be* by yourself alone, you must *inter-be* with the other person. This is why, in Plum Village, we say, "You are, therefore I am." We don't see an individual who suffers alone or who is happy alone. In the practice of mindfulness, not only do we try to remove the superiority and inferiority complexes; we try to remove the equality complex, too. As long as there is a self who's comparing, you will suffer.

But with the insight of interbeing, you don't compare anymore, because you know you are them and they are you; there is harmony, peace, and happiness.

THE WISDOM OF NONDISCRIMINATION

My right hand has written all of my poems except one, which was written on a typewriter using both my hands. Yet my right hand has never had a superiority complex. My left hand, although she has only helped write one poem and hasn't done any calligraphy at all, does not suffer from a inferiority complex.

One day I was trying to hang a picture on the wall. My left hand was holding a nail and my right hand a hammer. Instead of pounding the nail, I pounded a finger on my left hand. The left hand suffered, and right away the right hand put down the hammer and took care of the left hand in the most tender way, as though it was taking care of itself. The right hand didn't see it as its duty; it considers the left hand's suffering to be its own suffering. My right hand does not say: "I am me and you are you, we are different hands." In the same way, my left hand was not angry; it did not say, "Right hand, you have done me an injustice. Give me that hammer! I want justice!" Luckily, my two hands have the wisdom of nondiscrimination. They know they are one, not two. They know they inter-are, and there is no thought of revenge or punishment.

The wisdom of nondiscrimination is innate in us; it also exists in the other person. But if we allow wrong perceptions and habit energies to cover it up—the energies of individualism, self-centeredness, and selfishness, for instance—it cannot manifest. The practice of meditation helps us to recognize the seed of nondiscrimination in us. If we cultivate this seed and water it every day, it will manifest fully and liberate us.

RIGHT VIEW

When we listen to our own suffering, when we look deeply into the nature of our ill-being and our difficulties, we begin to have insight. We call that insight Right View.

We use the word "view," but more precisely we mean the abandoning of all views. We could say that Right View is no view. Right View removes all points of view, because truth cannot be described in these terms. A point of view is always partial. If we say that the elephant resembles a pillar because its leg is like a pillar or resembles a broom because its tail is like a broom, we don't see the whole truth; our point of view is limited and only allows us to see a part of the elephant.

With Right View, we discover the nature of interconnection and the interdependence of all things. We see that happiness and difficulty inter-are. Without difficulties, without suffering, we cannot be happy. Suffering is the compost from which the flowers of happiness grow.

LOOKING INTO THE RIGHT, YOU SEE THE LEFT

The truth of nonduality is apparent in all phenomena: left and right, above and below, good and bad, well-being and ill-being are all interconnected. Everything inter-is. When you look at the right, you can see the left; you cannot have one without the other. When you look at the ugliness, you can see the goodness and beauty.

This way of looking requires practice. We must look deeply into the ugliness to see the goodness. We must transcend our view in order to embrace, accept, and understand.

THE "OTHER SIDE"

Looking deeply, we realize that we have wrong perceptions about ourselves as well as about the "other side." We should try to remove our own wrong perceptions by listening to other political leaders—in Europe, in Asia, in Africa, and everywhere. Our own wrong perceptions lead to conflict, to suffering, and to war. In order to prevent war and violence, we need to transform wrong perceptions—both our own and the other side's. There is no other way.

THE REAL ENEMY

Our enemy is not outside of us. Our true
enemy is the anger, hatred, and discrimination
that is found in each of our hearts and minds.
We have to identify the real enemy and seek
nonviolent ways to remove it.

UNRAVELING THE CYCLE
OF HATRED

If we are able to see the sources of suffering
within ourselves and within the other person,
we can begin to unravel the cycle of hatred
and violence. When our house is on fire, we
must first put out the fire before investigating
its cause. Likewise, if we first extinguish the
anger and hatred in our own heart, we will
have a chance to deeply investigate the situation. We can then look with clarity and insight
to determine the causes and conditions that
have contributed to the hatred and violence we
are experiencing within ourselves and within
our world.

BEYOND PEACE NEGOTIATIONS

When there is a war raging inside us, it inevitably leads to a war with others. That is why going back to make peace within—within ourselves, within our group—is the basic peace practice.

If, in our own community or society, we can't listen to or understand each other, then how can we expect to listen to and understand other communities or nations? They suffer from fear, anger, and frustration, just like us. No matter how long we negotiate for peace, we cannot succeed as long as there is fear, anger, and frustration on both sides. This is why peace is not something that can be achieved by negotiation alone. First, peace comes by listening to ourselves—to our own suffering, our own difficulties—so that we can restore harmony within. When we have been able to listen to and embrace our own suffering, we allow it to transform, and then we communicate with the other side to help them do the same.

INSTRUMENTS OF PEACE

We should live our lives so that we contribute to our society's collective awakening. Our world situation is too important—too urgent—to be entrusted to politicians alone. We should help our political leaders to see the situation more clearly, to see that their present course of action is causing a lot of destruction, damage, and hate.

Violence does not work. If we want it to stop, we must use compassionate listening and gentle speech to remove the wrong perceptions that are at the foundation of hate and violence. We don't need instruments of violence like bombs and guns if we are able to use the instrument of deep, compassionate listening.

BEGIN RIGHT NOW

We can begin right now to practice calming our anger, looking deeply at the roots of the hatred and violence in our society and in our world, and listening with compassion in order to hear and understand what we have not yet had the capacity to hear and understand. When compassion begins to take shape in our hearts and minds, we begin to develop concrete responses to our situation. Once we have listened and looked deeply, we may begin to develop the energy of siblinghood between all nations, which is the deepest spiritual heritage of all religious and cultural traditions. In this way, the peace and under-standing within the whole world is increased day by day.

PRACTICES
FOR LISTENING

LISTENING TO THE BELL

Sometimes we need a sound to remind us to return to our conscious breathing. We call these sounds "bells of mindfulness." In Plum Village and the other practice centers in my tradition, we stop and listen whenever we hear the telephone ringing, the clock chiming, or the monastery bell sounding. These are our bells of mindfulness. When we hear the sound of the bell, we stop talking and stop moving. We relax our body and become aware of our breathing. We do it naturally, with enjoyment, and without solemnity or stiffness. When we stop to breathe and restore our calm and our peace, we become free, our work becomes more enjoyable, and the friend in front of us becomes more real.

Sometimes our bodies may be home, but we're not truly home. Our mind is elsewhere. The bell can help bring the mind back to the body. Because the bell can help us to go back to ourselves, back to the present moment, we consider the bell to be like a bodhisattva, a friend that helps us to wake up to ourselves again. With just three conscious breaths, we can release the tension in our body and mind and return to a cool, clear state of being.

In our tradition, we don't say "striking" the bell; we say, "inviting the bell to sound." The person who invites the bell is the bell master. We call the wooden stick that invites the bell, "the inviter." There are many kinds of bells: big bells that can be heard by the whole village or neighborhood; smaller bells that announce activities and can be heard all over the practice center; the bowl bell in the meditation hall that helps us with the practice of breathing and sitting; and the mini bell, a pocket-sized bell that we can bring along wherever we go.

Inviting the bell to sound, you breathe in and out deeply three times. If you enjoy breathing in and enjoy breathing out, then after three in-breaths and three out-breaths you become relaxed, calm, serene, mindful. You can recite this poem to yourself as you breathe in and out:

> *Listen, listen.*
> *This wonderful sound brings me back*
> *to my true home.*

"Listen, listen" means listen with all your heart when you breathe in. "My true home" is life, with all its wonders that are available in the here and the now. If you practice well, the Kingdom of God and the Pure Land of the

Buddha will be available whenever you go home to yourself with the sound of the bell.

If we're solid, awake, free, and mindful, then the sound of the bell that we offer can help people touch what is deepest within them.

Body, speech, and mind in perfect oneness,
I send my heart along with the sound of this bell.
May the hearers awaken from forgetfulness
and transcend the path of anxiety and sorrow.

The sound of the bell is the voice of the Buddha calling you back to yourself, back to the present moment, to your true home. Every time you hear it, you touch the Buddha nature within you. We take refuge in the present moment, in the island of self. We become more solid, more stable, and suffer less right away.

LISTENING TO THE BELL WITH YOUR CHILDREN

I have many friends, some very young, who love to practice inviting the bell and listening to the bell. In the morning before they go off to school, they sit down, they invite the bell to sound, and they enjoy breathing in and out. In this way, children can start the day with peace, serenity, and solidity. So instead of saying "have a good day" to your family members, you begin the good day together by breathing in and out with the sound of the bell. Before you go to sleep, you can sit down together as a family and practice breathing in and out together with the sound of the bell.

A young bell master should know that their in-breath and out-breath are shorter than the in-breath and out-breath of an adult. So after inviting the bell to sound, they should enjoy breathing in and out three times and then allow a little bit more time for the adults to fully enjoy their three in- and out-breaths. It's important that we can breathe mindfully by ourselves, but when the whole family breathes together, it creates a wonderful kind of energy that embraces everyone.

TELEPHONE MEDITATION

When the phone rings, the sound creates in us a kind of vibration, maybe some anxiety. "Who is calling? Is it good news or bad news?" There is a force that pulls us to the phone. We cannot resist. We are victims of our own telephone.

The next time you hear the phone ring, I recommend you stay exactly where you are, and become aware of your breathing: "Breathing in, I calm my body. Breathing out, I smile." When the phone rings the second time, you can breathe again. I am sure that this time your smile will be more solid than before. When it rings a third time, you can continue practicing breathing, while moving slowly to answer the phone. Remember you are your own master, dwelling in mindfulness. When you answer the phone, you know you are smiling, not only for your own sake but also for the sake of the other person. If you are irritated or angry, the other person will receive your negativity. But since you are smiling, how fortunate for them!

LISTENING TO OUR INNER CHILD

When we speak of listening with compassion, we usually think of listening to someone else. But we must also listen to the wounded child inside of us. Sometimes the wounded child in us needs all our attention. That little child might emerge from the depths of your consciousness and ask for your attention. If you are mindful, you will hear their voice calling for help. At that moment, instead of paying attention to whatever is in front of you, find a quiet place to go back and tenderly embrace the wounded child. You can talk directly to the child with the language of love, saying, "In the past, I left you alone. I went away from you. Now, I am very sorry. I am going to embrace you."

You can say, "Darling, I am here for you. I will take good care of you. I know that you suffer so much. I have been so busy. I have neglected you, and now I have learned a way to come back to you." Listen, and if necessary, you can cry together with that child.

Whenever you need to, you can sit and breathe with the child. "Breathing in, I go back to my wounded child; breathing out, I take good care of my wounded child."

You have to talk to your child several times a day. Only then can healing take place. Embracing your child tenderly, you reassure him that you will never let him down again or leave him unattended. The little child has been left alone for so long. That is why you need to begin this practice right away.

If you don't do it now, when will you do it?

LISTENING TO OUR ANCESTORS' VOICES

With practice, we can see that our wounded child is not only us. Our wounded child may represent several generations.

Our mother may have suffered throughout her life. Our father may have suffered. Perhaps our parents weren't able to look after the wounded child in themselves. So, when we're embracing the wounded child in us, we're embracing all the wounded children of our past generations. This practice is not a practice for ourselves alone, but for numberless generations of ancestors and descendants.

Our ancestors may not have known how to care for their wounded child within, so they transmitted their wounded child to us. Our practice is to end this cycle. The people around us, our family and friends, may also have a severely wounded child inside. If we've managed to help ourselves, we can also help them. When we've healed ourselves, our relationships with others become much easier. There's more peace and more love in us.

Go back and take care of yourself. Your body needs you, your feelings need you, your perceptions need you. The wounded child in you needs you. Your suffering needs you to listen and acknowledge it. Go home and be there for all these things. Practice mindful walking and mindful breathing. Do everything in mindfulness so you can really be there, so you can love.

TAKING CARE OF ANGER AND OTHER STRONG EMOTIONS

Our anger is like a small child crying out for their mother. When the baby cries, the mother takes them gently in her arms and listens and observes carefully to find out what is wrong. The loving action of holding her baby with tenderness already soothes the baby's suffering. Likewise, we can take our anger in our loving arms, listen, and feel relief right away.

We don't need to reject our anger. It is a part of us that needs our love and deep listening just as a baby does. After the baby has calmed down, the mother can feel if the baby has a fever or needs a change of diaper. When we feel calm and cool, we too can look deeply at our anger and see clearly the conditions allowing our anger to rise.

WALKING MEDITATION WHEN YOU'RE FEELING ANGRY

When you feel angry, it's best to refrain from saying or doing anything. You may like to withdraw your attention from the person or situation that is watering the seed of anger in you. Take this time to come back to yourself. Practice conscious breathing and outdoor walking meditation to calm and refresh your mind and body. After you feel calmer and more relaxed, you can begin to look deeply at yourself and at the person or situation causing anger to arise in you.

Walking meditation can be very helpful when you are angry. Try reciting this verse as you walk:

Breathing in, I know that anger is in me.
Breathing out, I know this feeling is unpleasant.

And then, after a while of walking meditation:

Breathing in, I feel calm.
Breathing out, I am now strong enough to
take care of this anger.

Until you are calm enough to look directly
at the anger, just enjoy your breathing, your
walking, and the beauty of the outdoors. After
a while, the anger will subside, and you will feel
strong enough to look directly at it, to try to
understand its causes, and to begin the work
of transforming it.

BELLY BREATHING

When a strong emotion arises, we say to it,
"You are only an emotion." An emotion is
something that comes, stays for some time,
and finally goes away.

Our person is made of our body, feelings,
perceptions, mental formations, and consciousness. The territory is large. You are much
more than just one emotion. This is the insight
you gain when a strong emotion comes up.
"Hello my emotion. I know you are there. I will
take care of you." You practice deep, mindful,
abdominal breathing, and you know that you
can handle the storm that has arisen in you.
You can sit down in a comfortable position
on the ground, or lie down. Put your hand on
your stomach, and breathe in very deeply,
breathe out very deeply, and become aware

of the rising and falling of your abdomen. Stop all thinking. Just be aware of your breath and the movement in your body. "Breathing in, my abdomen is rising. Breathing out, my abdomen is falling." Completely concentrate on the rising and falling of your abdomen. Stop all thinking, because the more you think about what has upset you, the stronger your emotion will become.

While practicing like this, don't allow yourself to stay at the level of your thinking. Bring your awareness down to the level of your breathing, just below the navel. Just become aware of the rising and falling of your abdomen. Stick to this, and you will be safe. It's like a tree in a storm: when you look at the top of the tree, you see the branches and leaves swaying violently back and forth in the wind. You may have the impression that the tree is going to break or be blown away. But when you bring your attention down to the trunk of the tree, you see how stable it is and you know that the tree is deeply and firmly rooted in the earth and can't be blown away. You know that the tree is going to withstand the storm. When you're engulfed in the storm of strong emotions, don't dwell at the top of the tree, at the level of thinking. Stop the thinking. Go down to the trunk, to your abdomen. Embrace the trunk and focus one hundred percent of your attention on the rise and fall of the abdomen. As long as you maintain mindful breathing, and focus solely on the rising and falling of your abdomen, you will be safe.

Don't wait until a strong emotion arises to begin this practice of mindful breathing or you will forget what to do when you need it most. We have to begin to practice right now, while the sky is clear and there are no storms on the horizon. If we practice for five or ten minutes every day, we'll naturally remember how to practice when we most need it, and we can survive the onslaught of a strong emotion very easily.

MINDFUL MEETINGS

Meetings can often be a source of tension, stress, and conflict, so in Plum Village we have certain practices to help us listen well to one another and maintain peace and harmony during meetings.

Before we start a meeting, we sit quietly and come back to ourselves. We listen to the sound of the bell to help us come back to our breathing and the present moment, calming our body and mind, and letting go of worries. Then we read a text to remind us to use loving speech and deep listening—to honor, respect, and be open to the views of others and to practice nonattachment to our own views. We know that the harmony of the community is the most important element for our collective happiness and that if we are attached to our present views, or try to impose them on others, we will create suffering. So we practice being open and listening to the experience and insight of others.

We invite everybody to express their ideas and we come to a consensus after we've heard everybody's views. We know that the collective wisdom and insight of the whole group is greater than the wisdom of any one individual. If we can't reach a consensus, we agree to discuss the matter again at a later time.

During the meeting, we practice using loving speech and deep listening. We let one person speak at a time; we never interrupt. While one person is speaking, the others all practice deep listening, trying to understand what the person wants to say. Deep listening means listening attentively to hear what the other person is saying and what is being left unsaid. We practice listening without judging or reacting. We don't get caught up in verbal duels. We speak from our own experience and address the whole group and if we have questions, we place the question in the center of the circle for the whole group to contemplate and address.

You might find it helpful to read the following text before you start a meeting or adapt it to suit your needs.

Meditation before a Meeting

We vow to go through this meeting in a spirit of togetherness as we review all ideas and consolidate them into a harmonious understanding—a consensus.

We vow to use methods of loving speech and deep listening in order to bring about the success of this meeting.

We vow not to hesitate to share our ideas and insights but also vow not to say anything when the feeling of irritation is present in us.

We are resolutely determined not to allow tension to build up in this meeting. If anyone senses the start of tension, we will stop immediately and come back to our breathing straight away, in order to reestablish the atmosphere of togetherness and harmony.

LISTENING TO YOUNG PEOPLE

As adults, we may think that we have lots of wisdom and experience, while children know very little because they are still young. Many generations of parents, teachers, and elder siblings have considered the opinions of children to be unimportant. They believe that they know what is best for the younger generation, but this is not necessarily true. When adults or elders haven't yet fully understood or listened deeply to the difficulties and the deep wishes of young people—their children, their younger siblings—they can't truly love them. Love has to come from understanding; when it doesn't, it is harmful. Without being aware of it, parents commonly cause their children to suffer in the name of love.

The most important thing is to keep communication alive. In a family, for example, we can have a weekly meeting between parents and children. Sitting together, we have an opportunity to discuss issues that are important for our happiness. If a child experiences a difficulty at school, or if the grown-ups have a dilemma in the workplace, it can be presented and the whole family can offer their insight into how to improve the situation. We don't have to call ourselves Buddhist to practice in this way. It's simply a matter of bringing peace and joy to our family and our community.

Loving speech and deep listening are two wonderful methods to open the door of communication with children; they are both crucial for this kind of meeting to be successful. If you are a parent, you should not use the language of authority but the language of love when speaking to your children. When you can speak with the language of love and understanding, your children will come to you and tell you their difficulties, suffering, and anxieties. With this kind of communication, you will understand your children better and be able to love them more. If your love isn't based on understanding, your children won't feel it as love.

To truly love, you can say to your child: "My love, do you think that I understand you well enough? Do you think that I understand your difficulties and your suffering? Please tell me. I want to know so that I can love you in such a way that doesn't hurt you." You can say, "Darling, please tell me the truth. Do you think that I understand you? Do I understand your suffering, your difficulties, and your deepest wishes? If I don't yet understand, then please help me to understand. Because if I don't understand, I'll continue to make you suffer in the name of love." This is what we call loving speech.

When your child is talking, please practice listening deeply. Sometimes your child will say something that surprises you. It may be the opposite of the way you see things. All the same, listen deeply. Please allow your child to speak freely. Do not cut them off as they are talking or criticize what they say. When you listen deeply with all your heart—for half an hour, one hour, or even three hours—you will begin to really see them, to understand them more deeply.

Related Titles by Thich Nhat Hanh

Happiness
How to Connect
How to Love
Reconciliation
Understanding the Mind

Monastics and visitors practice the art of mindful living in the tradition of Thich Nhat Hanh at our mindfulness practice centers around the world. To reach any of these communities, or for information about how individuals, couples, and families can join in a retreat, please contact:

Plum Village
33580 Dieulivol, France
plumvillage.org

Magnolia Grove Monastery
Batesville, MS 38606, USA
magnoliagrovemonastery.org

Blue Cliff Monastery
Pine Bush, NY 12566, USA
bluecliffmonastery.org

Deer Park Monastery
Escondido, CA 92026, USA
deerparkmonastery.org

European Institute of Applied Buddhism
D-51545 Waldbröl, Germany
eiab.eu

Thailand Plum Village
Nakhon Ratchasima
30130 Thailand
thaiplumvillage.org

Healing Spring Monastery
77510 Verdelot,
France
healingspringmonastery.org

Maison de l'Inspir
77510 Villeneuve-sur-Bellot
France
maisondelinspir.org

Asian Institute of Applied Buddhism
Ngong Ping, Lantau Island
Hong Kong
pvfhk.org

Nhap Luu-Stream Entering Monastery
Porcupine Ridge, Victoria 3461
Australia
nhapluu.org

Mountain Spring Monastery
Bilpin, Victoria 2758
Australia
mountainspringmonastery.org

Further Resources

For information about our international community, visit: plumvillage.org

To find an online sangha, visit: plumline.org

For more practices and resources, download the Plum Village app: plumvillage.app

THE THICH NHAT HANH FOUNDATION works to continue the mindful teachings and practice of Zen Master Thich Nhat Hanh, in order to foster peace and transform suffering in all people, animals, plants, and our planet. Through donations to the Foundation, thousands of generous supporters ensure the continuation of Plum Village practice centers and monastics around the world, bring transformative practices to those who otherwise would not be able to access them, support local mindfulness initiatives, and bring humanitarian relief to communities in crisis in Vietnam.

By becoming a supporter, you join many others who want to learn and share these life-changing practices of mindfulness, loving speech, deep listening, and compassion for oneself, each other, and the planet.

For more information on how you can help support mindfulness around the world, or to subscribe to the Foundation's monthly newsletter with teachings, news, and global retreats, visit **tnhf.org**.

PARALLAX
PRESS

Parallax Press, a nonprofit publisher founded
by Zen Master Thich Nhat Hanh, publishes
books and media on the art of mindful living
and Engaged Buddhism. We are committed to
offering teachings that help transform suffering
and injustice. Our aspiration is to contribute to
collective insight and awakening, bringing about a
more joyful, healthy, and compassionate society.

View our entire library at **parallax.org**.

The Mindfulness Bell, a journal of the art of mindful
living in the tradition of Thich Nhat Hanh, is published
two times a year by our community. To subscribe or to
see the worldwide directory of sanghas (local
mindfulness groups), visit **mindfulnessbell.org**.